Fun STEM Challenges

BUILDING SIMPLE TRAPS

by Marne Ventura

PEBBLE
a capstone imprint

Pebble Plus is published by Pebble, an imprint of Capstone.
1710 Roe Crest Drive, North Mankato, Minnesota 56003
www.capstonepub.com

Library of Congress Cataloging-in-Publication data is available on the Library of Congress website.
ISBN: 978-1-9771-1298-9 (library binding)
ISBN: 978-1-9771-1778-6 (paperback)
ISBN: 978-1-9771-1304-7 (ebook pdf)

Summary: Describes how to make a simple trap using a shoebox, tissue paper, and craft sticks.

Image Credits
Photographs by Capstone: Karon Dubke;
Marcy Morin and Sarah Schuette, project production;
Heidi Thompson, art director

Shutterstock: Ethan Daniels, 5, visionteller, 7

All the rest of the images are credited to: Capstone Studio/Karon Dubke

Editorial Credits
Erika L. Shores, editor; Juliette Peters, designer;
Eric Gohl, media researcher;
Laura Manthe, production specialist

All internet sites appearing in back matter were available and accurate when this book was sent to press.

Capstone thanks Darsa Donelan, Ph.D., assistant professor of physics, Gustavus Adolphus College, St. Peter, MN, for her expertise in reviewing this book.

Printed in China.
2493

Table of Contents

What Is a Trap?

Traps help people catch things.

If something goes into a trap,

it can't get out.

Why Build Traps?

Some traps are just for fun.

People make leprechaun traps.

Irish stories tell of these tricky fairies and their love of gold.

Can you make a leprechaun trap?

Make Your Own

Find a shoebox, paint, and
tissue paper. Gather craft sticks,
a small block, glue, and scissors.
Use coins and a small dish.

Glue tissue paper over an opening in the top of the painted box. Cut an X in the center. When something lands on the X, it falls down into the trap. It can't get out.

All traps need bait. It brings

something near a trap.

Gold would be a good bait to

catch leprechauns. Glue coins

behind the X you cut in the paper.

Traps need a way for things to get inside. Make a ladder. Ladders are inclined planes. They are simple machines. Inclined planes make it easier to climb up.

A see-saw is a lever. This simple machine moves things up and down. When the see-saw tips, something falls down into a trap. Would a leprechaun walk across a see-saw?

Use a toy figure or car. Push it up
the ladder and across the see-saw.
Can it go up the ladder easily?
Does the see-saw tip? Does the toy
fall in?

What Did You Learn?

A trap catches something. It can

be made using simple machines.

An inclined plane makes moving easier.

A lever tips weight up and down.

Glossary

bait—something used to make something come to a trap

inclined plane—a ramp that tilts at an angle

ladder—a structure with steps

leprechaun—a tiny fairy in Irish stories from a long time ago

lever—a bar that tilts up and down on a support piece called a pivot; a see-saw is a type of lever

simple machine—a tool with one or no moving parts that moves an object when you push or pull; inclined planes and levers are simple machines

trap—something used to catch and keep something

Read More

Juliano, Larissa. *How to Build an Elf Trap.* Naperville, IL: Sourcebooks Jabberwocky, 2018.

Rustad, Martha E. H. *Levers.* North Mankato, MN: Capstone, 2018.

Internet Sites

Green Kid Crafts: Leprechaun Trap
https://www.greenkidcrafts.com/leprechaun-trap/

Kids STEAM Lab
https://kidssteamlab.com/st-patricks-day-preschool-stem-activity/

The Best Ideas for Kids: Leprechaun Traps
https://www.thebestideasforkids.com/leprechaun-traps/

Critical Thinking Questions

1. Why do people use traps?

2. How can you make a trap with an inclined plane?

3. How does a lever help trap a leprechaun?

Index